Shifting Bone

———

Alison Malee

SHIFTING BONE

WRITTEN AND ARRANGED BY
ALISON MALEE

Cover Art by Aaron Slater

Cover Design by Mitch Green

www.alisonmalee.com

DEDICATION

To my incredibly selfless and supportive husband–
may our love bloom always.
To my ever growing daughter–
may you one day find me within these pages.
I love you both infinitely.

Cup your heart in your hands.

Whisper to your wounds,

"I am worthy."

CONTENTS

Shifting Bone

Seek

Seen

What is it to be known?
Will the ground open up to swallow me
or will it be a subtle falling?
Will my bones, my brittle servants,
snap beneath the weight of me
or will they stretch to meet the sun?
Will you pull me, pin me, stitch me
into a heavy weighted catalog of all that came before?
Or will this love be the infinite language
in which I learn to swim,
in which my lungs agree to listen once more
to the steady flow of air that sustains me?
What is it to be known, to be loved, to be seen?
Show me.

Heart

An infinite masterpiece–
the original heart of love.
Not marred by lust or greedy hands
but embedded with an endless outpouring
of one's glass into another's
without ever running dry.

Essential

Love is essential.
Nothing can exist without first being born of love.
It is the breath before a promise; a planted thing.
A wild flower at last settling roots into clean soil.
Love is the beginning and the end of all stories;
even those that have yet to be written.

Seeking

Eyes of loyalty.
Hands that do not crave.
Lips that know not of hunger;
I seek you.

Shall We?

Let's explore each other
like forbidden landscapes.
Hear the countries weep.
Listen to the foreign winds.
Answer the wildness in our skin.
Find our bones. Use our limbs.
Climb into each other.

Chorus

I am resting
on the curve of your lips.

I am resting
on the arch of your spine.

Pulling vowels
over my eyes

and waiting

to hear the choir scream
hallelujah.

Lung Capacity

I want you to feel love,
to know love,
and yet need my love
as if it allocates
the only air you dare to breathe.

Permanent

Your

tongue

is

the only

ghost

still

haunting

me.

Secret Keeper

With you I want to run
into the open arms of danger
and succumb to
the desperate secrets
I've failed to keep;
even from myself.

Here   and   There

Here, I can taste your promises
on the width of my tongue.
Melting honeysuckle and molasses.
Passing in waves and drifting
through the opal light of the wind.
Here, beneath the deepened soot of summer
I can taste your salt water skin, wet on my lips.
Here, before I was wordless and the poems began.
Here, we are light personified in the stillness.
We exist here, where we want to be seen.
We exist here, where we want to be known.
Where our skin is a mere paper covering and
our hearts are the gate keepers to our kingdom. Here.

Open Sky

You pull me.
A body
with no soul.

Spilling gold
beneath an
open sky.

Amber dust
scattered on
limbs.

Tangled in more than
heat and
lost in the
idea of
'stay'.

Only

You have allowed me to question
the darkest parts of my heart,
to imagine the world in a new light;
to dream beyond myself.
You have given me not only of yourself,
but also of the universe,
of the infinite glimpses of magic
that exist when I live with my eyes open.

Decorated

I will decorate you
in the shadows of tomorrows
yet to come and kiss away
your doubts about all your yesterdays.
I will love all your hidden,
tucked away corners,
I will soothe your aching wounds.
I will listen, always,
to what emerges from
your heart in the midst of your silence.

Knowledge is Power

And what of me, you say, who am I?
Why, you are the color of a watercolor sunrise,
of heavy cream poured
into an autumn morning.
Your breath smells of peace
and yet you rattle the very
essence of my bones.
You are living, breathing
fruit of the vine.
You are wine poured into
long stemmed glasses;
wine poured into me.
Drink and renew your
coursing wind and wildfire.
Drink of me and
know
of you.

Echoes

The door is open.

Will you remember here?
Will you remember now?
Maybe I am too full of
words to make room for silence.

Maybe I am too full of tongue and
lips and I cannot hear you over
my surrendering.

Music

Your hands are
writing and
revising
thick
black
honey
symphonies
along my spine.
Even the shadows
in your eyes
are songs
and oh, I have
heard you
sing, my love,
until your very
breath is poetry.

Your Name

We were scraped together by good intentions.
Held by strands of idle dreams
and lackluster ambitions.
Why, I didn't even know your name.
You were only skin and eyes
and we both knew better than
to grow fond of inanimate objects.

Need

We slept with our fingers interlaced,
beautifully woven together
like the sacred threads of time.

Heal

Why are you
folding yourself over
undoing your skin
to welcome love?
You are honey light.
Soft. Worthy.
Love should heal
your wounds
not create them.

-life lessons

In Shadow

Tonight the stars
burn ferociously against
this midnight canvas.

We lie beneath it all,
naught but two ineloquent humans
scrambling for answers.

Our faces lost in shadow,
our eyes dancing to the
thrum of our heartbeats
in the twilight.

Lush

It was evening, the kind
that is slow to come and leaves too soon.
You were sleeping next to me,
bathed in candlelight, lush and amber,
as I tried to fill these pages
with something of beauty.
But you were (you always are)
so distracting,
your chest rising and falling gracefully.
I could spend all of my years
on this frantic earth
watching the quiet pigments dance across
your skin, your lips, your eyes.
You were (are) magnificent.
I realized in that moment how
blessed we are that to us,
love is more than skin deep.
That to us
love sees more than color.
That to us
love embraces our differences
and calls it *beauty*.

Wisdom

The skin pulled snugly
against your chest
as the seasons changed.
I had never known a more
vivacious laughter than the sound
falling from your lips,
as time ticked
slowly on and the wisdom of the years
settled in for the winter.

Exist

My heart is no longer content with wandering.
For home exists in the smell of your skin,
in the swell of our hearts placed in each other's hands.

Quiet

I loved him in the quiet,
unseen places
and for all the ways
he caressed
my spirit with his words.

Recollection

Do you recall that day?
You smelled of fresh linens and bright, new beginnings,
and we were both dripping from the rain.
We had lived more in those searing moments
of liberation than most ever will.
It was then, both of us peering
out at the crowded city streets,
that I fell in love with
life once more.

Praises

If only
the seasons
wrote new
stories
on our
bones
the way
your laugh
seems to
praise the
earth for
blooming.

Lock and Key

Ah, but isn't that love?
Choosing with every passing day
to grow closer with only one person,
to hold only one hand,
to kiss only one set of lips.
Love anchors you;
but choosing to stay,
choosing is the key.

Saying

The words descended dizzily
from his lips and into the summer wind.
As if our sins could blow away,
as if his kisses did not imprint my skin,
as if I had not already spilled all of my brittle bones
at his feet and laid
my very essence at his fingertips.

All of You

His eyes dripped caramel;
oozed smoldering chocolate
and try as I might,
my mouth watered-
I could not look away.
I prayed for strength,
as my weaknesses
consumed me;
my inhibitions stolen by
the tangible
here, this, *now*.

Alison Malee

Dawn

Dawn melts into
sunrises.
Time slips.
Graceful,
between opened knees.
I ache like
the autumn wind
beneath your
steady hands.

Brilliance

I have held the infinite sun. It was you.

Simplicity

I like
the way
forever sounds
unfolding from
the center
of your
tongue.

Return

Returning

We will return.
Collect the
unbound
lush of
ourselves.

You bear the
grit in your throat
and I begin to
speak in truths.

We are learning
each other in waves.
Returning slowly.

We know there is never
an end (to us)

there is only an after.

Found

I seek you in the smell
of warmed vanilla.
In the spice of cinnamon.
I seek you in worn pages.
Crisp novels.
You move me, sweetly;
a song of warm air in the summer.
I seek you in bowing tidal waves,
in the melody of a lonesome robin.
I seek you in the canyon of my solitude,
where your candid smile
fills my lungs with longing—
but does not leave room for air.
Perhaps I should have loved you
enough to
make you
stay.

Soul

I have tasted the milk of the moon,
stolen like kisses from the center of
earth and placed upon my tongue.

The scent of the fading day
flutters like moth's wings down from
chimneys left too long in soot.

I drank, in gulps I could barely swallow,
a language lost but not forgotten.
Patient, waiting to part

my mouth from close.

The Sweetest Thing

The smell of your skin
lingers in the open air.
Lingers only to suffocate me;
to quell my good judgment
and bring me to my knees.

I know this isn't love, but
what it is tastes of sin and sugar,
breath and sunshine.

And oh, what delicacies I could find
wrapped between your legs,
wrapped inside your arms,
wound around your fingers.

We should get tangled
in this madness
and forget the world
outside our doors.

Tastebuds

The morning sunlight always coats
my waiting tongue with renewed hope
and thoughts of you.
Indulge in me.
Let me be the fragrant taste
your mouth desires.

Slow Burn

I have forged you of my nightmares;
dressed you in my dreams.
Will you set my soul ablaze
or will you empty me
of all that makes me burn?

When

Once
we were more
than this three-story walk-up,
and winter pressing
through windows, and
whispers of mistakes shared
by flickering candlelight.
Once we were more
than distracted conversations;
ice crystals forming along
lips left frozen
in silence.
Once.

Even Now

Still– I long for a permanent home
within your bloodied heart.
You, who have led me to the darkest of my hallows.
You, who made me of looking glass and shards of bone.
You. You swallow sagging grief to birth new life.
Still, my love. Even now.

Haunted

We danced together,
your ghost and I,
as the sun settled in
behind the weary clouds.
I could not feel the pressure of his skin,
or the warmth of his breath,
but I could feel him, love.
We danced until the birds
stopped singing and the sky
turned blue-black with the haze of dawn.
We danced until we could no longer
deny the rising sun his rightful place, and it was time.
Oh, how we dreaded the parting.
Yet I know we will dance again,
as surely as I know the wind
will carry him to me.
We will dance again,
we will love again,

your ghost and I.

S e c r e t s

How strange it is
to breathe your name
to life after years of
dusty *silence* perforated
only by the sound of
my pen to this
leather bound host of secrets.

Palms

Your hands
fall
heavy at
your sides.
You say
they are such
burdens.
Hands.
Always requiring
action.
I say
hands
allow you
to hold on.
To let go.
They are
my (your)
greatest
blessing.

Drifting

Stay afloat tonight.
Drift through
these murky seas
of memories
and hold my hand
as we weave
past the currents
and push through the waves.
Dive with me into this
empty abyss
of paper hearts,
and dream
until the old heavy warmth
of you burns me awake.

Cravings

I craved more
than this crash course,
fatal attraction,
kind of love,
but it has broken me
so whole heartedly
I can not *bear*
to go back for more.

Winding

I have begun dismissing
the manual labor of goodbyes,
and this evolution of tomorrows
where there is no you.
Oh, my weary heart
is a lonesome weight
wandering, suffocating
in the winding depths of solitude.

Sins

What sins you have committed with that tongue,
what thoughts you have evoked in me.
You taste of dark understanding; of citrus and burnt
honey,
of ancient heavenly impurities.
Why, to kiss your mouth, to bite your lips, you—
the sole proprietor of my destruction.
Oh, that is a cruel love.
Time and time again, my heart has betrayed me—
for only a savage, malicious beast could
feed my soul to you so willingly.

Ache

You have become a dull
ache in my bones.

A memory.

A locked door; a secret.

A love lost but never truly found.

Speaking

Silence speaks volumes;
of pages,
of chapters,
of novels,
of never ending distance
placed between family;
between friends,
between lovers.
But words..
Oh, words, how clumsily they fall;
dislodging from your throat
in a tumbling, dizzying down pour
of vowels
and syllables
and mistakes.
Words;
are sharper than a pinpricking needle
and quick pressure on a clean blade
and the burn of a lit cigarette against
delicate skin.
And the split second before a goodbye.

Heart

The language of creation
is not known to you yet.
It has been forming,
ever forming
on the width of your tongue.
Patiently
waiting for you to
remember your heart.

Truthful

For all the selfish ways
my heart has adopted,
I am still shrouded
by sympathy for all
of my past lovers.

Sweet Parting

In his wake, novels flourished within me
that I never knew could be written by my hands.
There is no greater parting gift.

Hurt

Far Enough

It pulls and it aches
and the muscles clench
so tightly my lungs cave in
on themselves in longing.
You are so
far,
far,
far from me.
Always out of reach;
yet, never far enough to stop
my haunting daydreams.

Wait

I watched as the sea
rose up to drown us.
As the waves,
such beautiful creatures,
swallowed our bodies;
bitterly devouring and
spitting out our fragile bones.
I watched as our hearts
fought ever so valiantly,
yet,
even those
betrayed us in the end.

Stars

...a desire
that is
whispered only
to ourselves
when the night
has grown
cold and the
stars are
weeping too.

Lost

We have been lost to the ocean.
Oh, high tides,
I pray you,
show mercy.
For all my lack of oxygen,
I do believe these waters
have such eyes,
and do take pride
in silencing me
beneath the currents;
swallowing us in the waves.

Entrapment

If only words could express the constant battle
between loyalty and freedom,
perhaps my heart would
stop yearning for more
and learn to live in this cage of contentment.
The inescapable walls of everyday hum drum.
And this terror that I've begun to associate with breathing
would not feel as heavy or loaded or dismal.
If only words could express
the war plummeting through my veins and into
my heart and pounding through my skull
and keeping me alive and yet killing me slowly.
Locked in this prison;
content to keep secret the love affair
I am having with this beautiful world.
What does one have to do to
break
free?

Shattered

A shattered soul
looks a lot like
a human on a
Wednesday.
A nameless,
ageless face
disappearing
behind years of
deliberate smiles.

Drown

I want to dry the
ocean of him,

quench his thirst
for the world.

Sometimes I think he is my
saving grace,

sometimes I hear his name
and drown.

Human

As if I can reach out and
run my fingers through
the disastrous parts of my soul
and feel it pulse with warmth
and life and the remnants of my sanity.
I can hear the echoes
rattle through my bones;
and I cannot decide if it delights or terrifies me.
I am only **human**.
Merely sewn together
with brilliant promises
and the fearful hope
that tomorrow will be a *better* day.

Can You See Me?

I am bound by insecurities
and the naive prayer
that no one can see them.

Voice

What more of me
can be woven
back into my spine
back behind skin
back behind bone
back where no one
can hear
my voice
at all.

Where

I remember you.
Even when I close my eyes.
And cannot remember me
back to myself.

My Fears

As for me, I am wrapped in heavy fears,
strung together like underbrush soaked
in gasoline, waiting for an open flame.
A threatening, perilous thing.

Order

I understand chaos.
Chaos grounds me to this earth,
to the pressure of immediacy.
It is order that leaves me feeling distant,
that hinders my pulsing connection to the universe.

Uncharted

My heart tugs me into uncharted waters,
wrapping me in quiet assurances, and I–
I must admit, some days
I am propelled by my desires,
and others I am surrounded,
unable to hold my head above the foaming sea.

Impatience

My voice– a howling creation,
echoes against the brutality of winter;
a cry which has exposed me
to the biting frost of days that
drift into eternities.

When did the sun last
heat the ground,
last bring life to this sunken
landscape?

Oh, this impatient roar
hath torn me asunder.
I am emptied of me.

Storm

I have come to know fear
as well as I know my own quivering heart–
wholly, as a smoldering storm knows the rain.

Sew

Your fingers
sew me
eloquently.
Foreign lace.

Run
quick
beneath my
veins.
A river of
sunflowers you
buried here.

I ride the currents,
while you
make a map
of me.

Heavyweight

We carry with us such burdensome
lifetimes of abandonment and
still we manage to love
with the ferocity of untamed wild things.

Ebony

We are
stark white
and ebony
hands
both
pressed to glass
too sharp to hold
but small enough
to grasp

if only for a moment.

Too Much

There is too much of me
that has been scattered to the wind.
Too many pieces engulfed
by a universe spun softly.
What will become of me,
when all of me
has gone?

Open

You spill open.
Clean
against this
navy dusk.

Your tongue,
your hands,
race
sharp
down the edge of me.

The sky
drips heavy
nectar at my feet.

And I see you,
purely.

How did I not know?

Even the
innocent have
teeth.

Vitality

What is more vital than your heart?
Which pumps life through you.
Why do you insist on the shattering?
The build and rebuild.
The cover and uncover.
One day you will miss a fragment.
In the shuffle.
A small piece. A section of yourself.
This is how.
The hurt grows.
When skin is stitched.
Over empty places.
This is how.
Scars are born.

How?

It is a tender flesh
that I am made of.
I bruise, I shatter
with the smallest
breath of wind.
In the breaking,
I have searched
for me, but there
are too many
quiet ways
in which I have
somehow forgotten
myself.

Lifetime

You can spend years.
A lifetime.
Locked in your head.
Feeding your demons.
But they. Are not real.
And you. Deserve more
than a cage built by your own hands.
Do not. Breathe life. Into your fears.

From My Mouth

What am I to do when the words come.
And my jaw unhinges?

Wiring

I was wide awake beneath
the timid shadows of the willow tree,
my thoughts humming between
the space of maybe and the hope of possibility.

I existed solely of frayed wires and passionate embraces,
burning electricity with the force
of a thousand swinging chandeliers.

But the shadows only lingered for so long;
as this trembling tree is that which protected
me from none other than myself.

Lavender

Our room is
collecting dust.
Long overdue,
ghost town.

Your hands embrace
the concept of forgiveness—
two lovers caught
playing with wolves.

Oh, you are your father's son.
All smoke,
and no perception of time.

Your smoldering tongue
and those cigarette words
could pursue,
could capture me.

Almost.

Maybe.

Discover

Teetering

Shaking hands
this morning
found strength
in earl grey
and words
written by someone
much wiser than I.

Frost coats the windowpane,
freezing time;
and for an
infinite moment

I drift in silence.

Fully Lived

I want a life of magnificent chaos.
Sweet children, busy years, and happy days.
A place to call my own in this world,
and a desk full of work I have spilled my soul into.
I want a life brimming
with kind hearts, and relentless love.
I want a life fully imagined, and fully lived.

Speak

I speak in love.
A language that often
leaves me tongue tied.

Roam

My daydreams are free to roam
on the off chance that someday
they will collide with reality.

Sleeve

A soft
memory
pulling on your
sleeve.

Syrup in your words.

Watching the rich
language of time
parting lips,
passing through.

Paper and
light
both fading
with age.

Returning Home

I am beginning to understand
the way my bones settle.
I have been,
my whole life through,
a vagabond.
It is only now, as I feel my breath
move through me like a steady,
coursing river that I am
finally coming home.

Sometimes

Sometimes the words
call me from sleep
and the poems
speak their way to paper.

Sometimes I am not
involved in the creation.

Sometimes I am a vessel
for the universe.

Similarities

The evening stretched into dawn,
like arms over head on a
muted Sunday morning.
We sat together but apart,
knees pulled in tight to
our chests, and spoke of all

the dreams we weren't too sure would come to pass.

We locked eyes and looked away.
Locked eyes and watched the dust settle,
as if we could not feel the heat rising
to our timid cheeks.
The night had grown tired of us
and the moon had settled into sleep.
Still, we swung our feet down from wobbly chairs,
and padded, soft, to the kitchen
listening to the drip of coffee brewing,
surprised to hear a heartbeat so similar to our own.

Heat

There is lavender
between your words
and heat in your voice.

How fragile this life
is nestled in
your own
quiet heartbeat.

Introductions

I do not know
if I am ready
to meet myself
quite yet.
I have become
and been undone
too many times
to be certain
we will make
a good
first impression
on each other.

Fumbling

Our human tongues can
only fumble for truth for but so long,
before we understand
that the absence of sound transcends
our attempts at carving stars with our words.

Silence carries with it the
immense weight of beauty.

Hand in Hand

It has always been freedom
that handed me the courage
to unravel myself from my own destruction.

Beginning

Poetry exists within the cautious frame
of terror and understanding.
Within the spilled blood of all who came before.
Held in each ink-stained hand
to selflessly pick up a pen and begin.

Between

How will you choose
between this, here,
and the taste
(lips, eyes, her)
of freedom.

Cruelty

I have held my tongue in anger.
I have held my tongue in fear.
I have remained
silent
silent
silent
and I think that is far too
cruel a fate for my words.

Directions

I am but a ghost,
hung by the ornate tapestries
of my own failures;
a spirit haunted by the prose
I have not written.
There are days I fear
I may lose myself entirely
to the maze of my mind;
searching for a sweeping
landscape of grace to call home.

Pen to Page

To be a writer is
to know great solitude.
To find peace in consuming silence.
It is to be as comfortable with
the whispers in your mind
as you are with your own voice.
It is to be patient, humble, and irrevocably human.
One is a writer when one must write;
when the pull to put pen to paper
is as permanent as the desire to breathe.

Realizations

When I am utterly *lost* in the words,
hidden deep within the secluded pages
of a tenderly dressed novel–
that is where I find myself.

Grace

Grace is soft, gentle.
A dandelion floating
as it turns the milky hue
of changing seasons.
A small child splashing
in the waves without fear.
Oh, I imagine Grace to feel
like the tender flesh of a mother's bosom;
smelling of sweet nectarines
hidden in the neat rows of an orchard.
For what is Grace, if not a poem nestled
on the tip of your tongue in the morning?
Humbling us by the beauty of her existence.

Ink and Heart

When you write,
you bleed a little piece
of your soul onto the page
and pray your readers will look after it.

Bones

Whisk me away, spread me thin
across the galaxies so I may drink
in the echoing symphonies evolving
from my love of words.

Within these wild, breathing stars
I feel I may be free to embrace the songs
that have welled and poured
from the coiled marrow of my bones.

With You

There is with you
the sacred
(that clings)
the fragrance of you.
How my skin
hot
blushes
beneath your fingers.
The cave
the savoring
of smooth muscle
beneath pressure.
How did you know you could
(would)
find my woman curves
concealed in this
fragile surrendering.
When I did not even
yet know what I was
becoming.
(whole)
-the first

Only If

Speak
only if your words are
steeped in honey
my wounds
are sore
salt soaked
desperate for
healing.

Coloring

What is the color of silence,
for I have seen its water color
markings around the door.
Felt it whisper hot on my cheek.
It has painted my solitude in meaning
and draped me in the everlasting breath of life.
The nourisher of my soul,
the inhabiter of light and shadow.
Silence has moved me,
as only time has moved
the shallow waters of the sea.
Yet it remains hidden,
perhaps somewhere
between the here and now.
Perhaps beyond.
To seek it out has
always been reckless,
but ah, to chance upon it.

Storyteller

How might I begin this
long awaited chapter, but to tell you
of the boundaries of my humanness?
I am both flesh and spirit, mind and body,
merging, colliding, fading into sunsets of delicate
bones and insatiable passion.
It is almost unfathomable
to separate the two,
for though I am but one person,
I am of the Earth
and of Heaven and Hell
and I exist as a delicate

collision of all that fills me.

At Peace

I am at peace with my doubt.
It gnaws at me when I am unsure.
When I am creating.
When I am writing.
When I am searching for truth.
But I have learned to be still, to listen;
and sometimes, to risk it all anyway.
To leap.

Smoke

Poetry unwinds from my blue-black veins,
a billow of heavy smog, pouring, winding, into life.

Golden

Faint traces of gold still swim
in my bloodstream from my younger
years when money was cheap and
love was the only necessity.

Wilting

Oh, words.
Embedded helplessly into my withered fingers.
Words that have poisoned the tongues of many
and flavored the thoughts of few.
For although they decorate pages
with good intentions,
there are still flowers that bloom
and wilt aloft my pen strokes.

Intoxicated

Have you
ever
sauntered
into
a poem
and
stumbled
out drunk
on
understanding?
This is
art.

The Split

I have ended
my relationship
with Doubt.

She worries too much.

Skin

I adore the pale sky.
The blushing hues of noon.
The deepened black of night.
Canvases say naught
without variations of living color.

Midnight

The moon caresses my secrets tenderly,
like a lover's hand she has never known
but always missed.
I so admire her gentleness,
for I have swallowed
two halves of a whole sky
solely to cleanse
my reeking bones of their desires.

Passing Time

I walk this Earth
both tethered to the moon
and planted on the sun.
I am but a humble servant to the sea,
bathed in flesh,
and fearful of the hands of time.

Meaning

These words are of my soul;
soaked in my own blood.
They are stark as bone and weak as flesh.
Heavy, and transparent with meaning.

These words are all I have to give you.

Today

Such mystery lies in daybreak.

As if the earth is ending
and beginning in a moment.

Acknowledging

All the words I wished to say
grew like wild flowers in my throat,
until every time I moved my lips
a garden tumbled forth and
I had to learn to speak.

-the blossom

August

Sometimes.
I speak to the moon.
She teaches me of love.
I teach her of humanity.

Existence

I am

I am

I am

and I

must

never forget.

Become

Options

Give yourself the freedom to make mistakes.
There is no excuse for foolishness,
but there is for unbridled curiosity.

Honesty

Unleash your mind—
be the kind of honest that
terrifies the ordinary.
That startles the sleeping
and awakens the dead.
Breathe into yourself,
and love your dark
corners,
your brightly lit windows
until you have *become*.
Until the truth of you has
blossomed
fully into
existence.

Truly

To see a man be honest
(truly)
water soaked in his
vulnerabilities
may be one of the most
beautiful human
experiences.

Inside of Me

Love,
hiding inside your head
will not keep the world
from turning.
Abandon logic;
abandon reason,
and embrace the dark space
within you that
holds on to your dreams.
These arms are spread wide,
waiting for you to
come home to your
sense of adventure.
Where have you been?

Lovely

You are blushing
wild flowers into existence.
Alive with sun.
Ripe with honey fruit,
sweet and full.

You do not need to speak.
I can see love writing
its language on your lips.

Importance

The voice that rises up
from your throat
is the only validation
you need that your opinion matters.

Vow

There is a yesterday
too full of abuse (self)
to speak of.
Today I promise (vow)
to speak tenderly.
To be tender.
To remember.
I matter, too.

Reminder

Let your heart settle.
Rub rose oil on your bruises.
Scent the air with salt.
Be present with your pain.
Remind yourself–
(more than once if necessary)
it is okay to shatter.

Even the sky weeps.

Details

Do not focus on the details of your insanity.
Life is much too short to linger
on the how and why behind your genius.

Self

I appreciate myself. That is how I heal.

Forgiveness

Choose, everyday, to forgive yourself.
You are **human**.
Flawed.
Most of all,
you are worthy of love.

Change

I have changed.
Ten-fold.
Grown out of my skin.
Become *woman*.
Tasted the air
as a new being.
Sang as the moon
chased me from the shore.
In every way–
I am ready for
magic.

Settle

My heart often
wonders about you.
Where did you go
and where are you now?
Did the leaving
set you free?

Kindness

Ah, kindness.
What a simple way to tell
another struggling soul
that there is love to be found in the world.

Just So

Just so
I stay here.
Whole.
Unopened.

Just so
there is ginger in my hair,
sun in my skin.
My hands dip
into rich soil.
I am blending into
this war in my belly.

Just so
color dots my cheek.
Now (always) I learn
to grow flowers
where there is no rain.
To grow gardens
in the midst
of a storm.

Power

Be soft but unafraid to conquer.

Own

I am
wise now.

Full of breath
that
belongs only
to me.

Seeds of Truth

Seeds of truth
I take

taste

swallow.

Feel them soothe
the ignorance
coiled in my throat.

Chamomile tea
sip
calm the aching.
Spit out
the fear of the unknown.

I have been
bleeding
bleeding
bleeding
for a world too
long lost in midnight
to see the light of dawn.

What Matters

As women, we must learn
to view ourselves as more
than skin and flaws and bones.
Our beauty comes from
the power of our minds,
the courage of our hearts,
the strength of our voices.
We are more.
We *are* more.

Courage

It takes great courage
to let your mind,
your body,
your soul wander
into the unknown.
Surrender to the
wilderness within you.

Forever

Shroud me in daylight,
etch me into the glowing aftermath of this,
our most tender embrace.
We are chasing infinity.
We are catching the sunrise of a new day.
Because what exists beyond the walls
of our uncertainty
is a possible forever.

Gardening

It is your duty to plant roots,
to be unafraid of the infinite.
You have been created beautifully—
wild and seamless.
It is your duty to define yourself
not by your failures,
but by how well your seeds have been tended to;
how well you have fed your soul.

Your spirit was designed for magnificence.

Beauty

The mirror cannot see your soul,
nor the ways your heart is set ablaze.
So here is a reminder
that you are human and you are beautiful.

Denial

Do not deny yourself.
Even the dusty corners
you forgot to clean
(maybe tomorrow?)
are lovely.

Everything

Everything that is,
and is to come,
is temporary.
Love. Hatred. Fear. Life.
Embrace all there is,
and when the time comes, let it go.

We Must

When did we become unable
to address the lull in our own heartbeats
as we sit around the table, bowing our heads to pray?
How have we allowed our hearts
to swell and spill with empathy,
but our ears to remain closed off by ignorance?
We.
Cannot create change.
Without first.
Changing.

Freedom to Begin

What allows you to breathe? Do that.
You do not need to ask for permission.

Roar

Peace should not be quiet.
It should roar from the heavens
and drench our lands in hope.

Wisdom

You are a lush and beautiful
outpouring of soul.
You are a limitless sky.
Why do you speak softly?

Bloom

Bloom
honestly
and
with
intention.

Ask Yourself

Tell me your story.
Where do you begin?
What have you created?
Are you free?

Who are They?

They say we know not of beauty

but

we

feel every color awakening,

we

see silence as the dawn appears,

we

capture the night to resurrect the stars,

we

are more than savage bones

and

they

know not of us.

-Who are we?

Dear Human,

You are a home
a steady hand
a love letter to yourself
a soft echoed utterance

a revolution.

Unanswered Prayers

I pray these prayers of soft tissue and plump flesh.
I pray these prayers that have been held close for too
long,
that smell of worn skin and buttered warmth.
Please, let us find our way.
Let us learn to cherish our brothers.
Let us learn to cherish out sisters.
Speak to our hearts.
Let us know that we are not so different.
Let us know that we all beat with the same blood.

We all beat with the same blood.

Sacrifice

If you must breathe–
breathe softly.
Be tender.
Your body bears the weight of you.

Miracles

& maybe today is the
start of something.
Maybe by you just
waking up this morning,
you have set in motion a series
of beautifully complicated miracles.

Unwanted

When you start to need a person.
Many people.
To fill you.
To validate you.
It is because.
You have gone unwanted by yourself.
For too long.

Self Love

The only
cure
I have
ever known
for
fear and
doubt and
loneliness
is an
immense
love
of
self.

Limited

You are not limited to 'beautiful'.
You are not limited to 'pretty'.
You are made of too much
'powerful' to even consider it.

Comfort(able)

Be kind to your body.
You are learning
what it means
to become more than
a roof
a wall
a ceiling.
You are becoming
a woven tapestry
of
comforts;
a home
to yourself.
It takes time.

The Rise

A dark song rises from my lips.
Steam from a smoldering kettle.
December's early morning icy fog.
A song of womanhood,
which of all things has draped me
in these hips and gifted me my fertile womb.
I can hear the melody, succulently sweet.
It spills from me, the rise and fall of notes
cascading from my breath and into the world.
It is not my own. It is of me, and of you,
and of all my sisters dancing
through these bouts of life.
Our blood runs through it, a river,
a song; a renewal of self.
Of great light and conceived
of such darkness, the song rises.
We rise.

Shifting Bone

I am woman.
I am womb and breast.
I am sloping hips.
I am flowing milk.
I am creation;
I bring life to barren land.
I am born of strength and
shifting bone.
I am born of woman,
robed in beauty and humility.
I am as real as the breath of
my own pulsing lungs.
I am sacred as the dance of the breeze.
I am all I am,
for me, for her-
for you.

This book is for you, dear reader.

You have shown me such kindness, such compassion, and such utter support.

I love you.

Thank you for being tender with my heart.

ACKNOWLEDGEMENTS

A huge thank you to my husband, who spent so much
time listening to me grumble about editing, deadlines, and
the crippling fear that this book wouldn't be successful.
Thank you for your loving spirit, your endless pep talks,
and being my complete support system. You amaze me
everyday. Thank you to all of the amazing artists that
have collaborated to make this book the beauty that it is.
All of you are immensely talented and
I am honored that you let me showcase your artwork in
this collection. Thank you to all of the beautiful people at
Evolver Social Movement for your incredible support. I
am so grateful for all of you. Thank you to my family for
your love through this process, and your patience with me
when I am locked away writing for days on end.

Alison Malee

Author

Alison is a writer, poet, mother, and lover of
caffeinated beverages. She currently resides
in New York City with her daughter and
husband, and is working on her second
collection of poetry.

www.alisonmalee.com

Instagram: alison.malee

Aaron Slater

Cover Artist

www.aaronslaterdesign.com

Robert Dean

Interior Artist

www.robertdeanstudios.com

www.watercolorwedding.com

Instagram: robertdean.art

ALISON MALEE

www.alisonmalee.com

CPSIA information can be obtained
at www.ICGtesting.com
Printed in the USA
BVOW10s1819120916
461895BV00010B/79/P